WHERE NATURE SHINES

LA TERRE OÙ LA NATURE S'ÉCLATE

WO DIE NATUR ZU HAUSE IST

WHERE NATURE SHINES
LA TERRE OÙ LA NATURE S'ÉCLATE
WO DIE NATUR ZU HAUSE IST

Photographs / Photographies / Fotos © Sigurgeir Sigurjónsson 1999
Text / Texte / Text © Ari Trausti Guðmundsson 1999
English translation: Anna Yates
Traduction française: Catherine Eyjólfsson
Deutsche Übersetzung: Helmut Lugmayr
Design / Conception / Design: Anna Cynthia Leplar
Printing / Impression / Druck: Nørhaven a/s, Denmark

FORLAGIÐ · Reykjavík · 2005

ISBN English 9979-53-368-4
     Français 9979-53-375-7
     Deutsch 9979-53-374-9

Sigurgeir Sigurjónsson
Ari Trausti Guðmundsson

WHERE NATURE SHINES

LA TERRE OÙ LA NATURE S'ÉCLATE

WO DIE NATUR ZU HAUSE IST

FORLAGIÐ

In modern, advanced societies, more and more people suddenly remember an old truth: We are all part of nature. We have to live from nature in harmony with nature.

Consequently, an increasing number of people seek refuge, knowledge and peace in nature. In many industrialised countries, one has to search long and hard for a subtle companionship with nature. Man's activities have made their mark on vast areas and pushed back the borders where untamed nature is at hand to the more remote areas and faraway countries.

In Europe, the many nature reserves and much fewer unspoilt areas become increasingly popular. At the fringes of the continent, Iceland still has much to offer. About half its area is a wilderness, dotted with rare or beautiful natural phenomena and constituting vast, clean spaces, so refreshing for our soul and body. The other half, outside towns, is sparsely inhabited countryside where nature greets visitors in varied and splendid forms.

In the geological sense, Iceland is among the youngest landmasses in the world. The forces of its creation are still at large; every fourth year on average, another volcanic eruption adds new areas to the island and hot springs bubble or hiss in

many regions . Ripping motions of crustal movements may open up fresh fissures and cracks. Relentless natural forces tear the bedrock down at the same time: vast glaciers, fierce rivers, battering oceanic waves and the grinding work of wind-blown sand and frost or thaw. All this unfolds in the open before our eyes and one can rest assured; all visitors may feel as safe in Iceland as the Icelanders themselves have done for centuries.

Iceland is not only an El Dorado for those interested in landscape or hard rocks - its nature is full of life. Lush areas with birch forests and colourful vegetation greet the eye. Millions upon millions of birds fill the air, especially  along the coastline. There, abundant sea mammals are seen at sea and on the beaches. Rivers and lakes teem with salmon and trout and reindeer and foxes roam the highlands.

So, meet nature in Iceland and savour what you sense.

Dans les sociétés modernes et avancées, de plus en plus de gens se remémorent soudain une ancienne vérité : nous faisons tous partie de la nature. Nous devons en vivre, mais en harmonie avec elle.

Il s'ensuit qu'un nombre croissant de gens cherchent désormais refuge, savoir et paix dans la nature. Dans bien des pays industrialisés, on peut chercher loin et longtemps avant de trouver cette compagnie subtile de la nature. L'activité de l'homme a laissé sa marque sur de vastes régions et repoussé les limites de la nature sauvage à des territoires éloignés et à des pays lointains.

En Europe, les nombreuses réserves naturelles et les zones vierges, bien plus rares, attirent de plus en plus de visiteurs. Située à la limite du continent, l'Islande a encore beaucoup à offrir. Près de la moitié de sa superficie à l'état sauvage, ponctuée de phénomènes naturels d'une rare beauté, représente de vastes espaces vierges qui font du bien au corps et à l'âme. L'autre moitié du pays, en dehors des agglomérations, est une campagne peu peuplée où la nature accueille le visiteur sous ses formes les plus variées et les plus belles.

Sur le plan géologique, l'Islande compte parmi les terres les plus jeunes du monde. Les forces qui l'ont créée sont toujours à l'œuvre : tous les quatre ans en moyenne, une nouvelle éruption volcanique accroît la surface de l'île tan-

dis que les sources chaudes bouillottent et sifflottent ci et là. L'écartèlement de la croûte terrestre peut ouvrir de nouvelles lézardes et fissures. Les forces de la nature effritent dans le même temps le socle rocheux par le jeu sans répit des vastes glaciers, des rivières indomptées, des coups de boutoir des vagues et par le travail d'usure des tempêtes de sable, de l'alternance du gel et du dégel. Tout cela se déploie sous nos yeux, et pourtant, qu'on se rassure : les visiteurs n'ont pas plus à craindre que les Islandais eux-mêmes au cours des siècles.

L'Islande n'est pas seulement un pays de Cocagne pour ceux qui aiment les paysages et les roches dures, car sa nature est pleine de vie. Des zones colorées de végétation luxuriante et de bois de bouleaux réjouissent le regard. L'air de la côte vibre du cri de millions d'oiseaux. On aperçoit des mammifères marins près du rivage et sur les plages. Rivières et lacs regorgent de saumons et de truites, tandis que rennes et renards hantent les hauts plateaux.

Il faut venir goûter aux sensations rares d'une rencontre avec la nature islandaise.

In modernen, entwickelten Gesellschaften entdecken heute immer mehr Menschen wieder eine alte Weisheit: Wir alle sind Teil der Natur. Wir müssen von der Natur und im Einklang mit der Natur leben.

Als Folge davon machen sich viele auf, um Zuflucht und Entspannung in der Natur zu suchen, aber die Suche nach einer intensiven Verbundenheit mit der Natur ist in vielen industrialisierten Ländern langwierig und mühevoll geworden. Die Aktivitäten der Menschen haben weiten Gebieten ihren Stempel aufgedrückt und die Grenzen, an denen man unberührter Natur begegnen kann, immer weiter in abgelegene Gebiete und weitentfernte Länder verschoben.

Die zahlreichen Naturschutzgebiete und wenigen noch ursprünglich erhaltenen Landstriche Europas erfreuen sich zunehmender Beliebtheit. Am Rande des Kontinentes hat Island noch viel davon zu bieten. Ungefähr die Hälfte des Landes ist unbewohntes Hochland, in dem sich seltene und faszinierende Natur-

phänomene verbergen und das einen hervorragenden Platz zur Erholung für Leib und Seele bietet. Die andere Hälfte des Landes wird, von den Städten einmal abgesehen, von kleinen ländlichen Siedlungen geprägt, in denen der Besucher der Natur auf viel-fältige und abwechslungsreiche Weise begegnen kann.

Geologisch gesehen gehört Island zu den jüngsten Landmassen der Erde. Die

Kräfte, die die Insel geschaffen haben, sind noch immer am Werk; alle vier Jahre im Schnitt fügt ein neuer Vulkanausbruch dem Land weitere Teile hinzu, und heiße Quellen sprudeln oder zischen an vielen Stellen hervor. Bei ruckartigen Bewegungen der Erdkruste können sich neue Risse und Spalten öffnen. Gleichzeitig wird das Gestein von den unbarmherzigen Kräften der Natur wieder abgetragen: riesige Gletscher, reißende Flüsse, brandende Wellen und das Zusammenspiel von Wind und Sand sowie der Wechsel von Wärme und Frost formen die Landschaft. All das entfaltet sich direkt vor Ihren Augen und erlaubt es Ihnen, die Wunder der Natur in Ruhe und Geborgenheit zu bestaunen; jeder Besucher kann sich in Island ebenso sicher fühlen, wie es die einheimische Bevölkerung seit Jahrhunderten getan hat.

Island stellt nicht nur ein Eldorado für jene dar, die sich für Landschaften und hartes Gestein interessieren, sondern die Natur ist voller Leben. Üppige Hänge mit Birkenwäldern und farbenfroher Vegetation erfreuen das Auge. Millionen und Abermillionen von Vögeln erfüllen die Luft, vorallem entlang der Küsten, an denen man eine Unmenge von Meeressäugetieren im Wasser und an den Stränden beobachten kann. In den Flüssen und Seen tummeln sich Lachse und Forellen und Rentiere und Füchse durchstreifen das Hochland. Besuchen Sie Island und geniesen Sie mit allen Sinnen, was seine Natur zu bieten hat.

1 The church at Selárdalur in Arnarfjörður, the site of famous witchhunts in the 17th century.

L'église de Selárdalur dans le fjord d'Arnarfjörður; lieu historique lié à des affaires de sorcellerie au 17e siècle.

Die Kirche in Selárdalur im Arnarfjörður. Ein
geschichtlicher Ort, der u.a. während der
Hexenverfolgungen im 17. Jh. bekannt wurde.

Kirkjan í Selárdal við Arnarfjörð; sögufrægur
staður m.a. vegna galdramála á 17. öld.

2 Rauðisandur on Barðaströnd. The beach consists largely of pale shell-sand.

Rauðisandur sur la côte de Barðaströnd. Le sable doit sa couleur claire aux débris de coquillages.

Rauðisandur in den südlichen Westfjorden.
Die Sandbänke bestehen zum größten Teil aus
hellem Muschelsand.

Rauðisandur á Barðaströnd. Sandurinn er að
mestum hluta ljósar skeljaleifar.

3   The view from Mt. Námafjall over Hlíðardalur   Vue des hauteurs de Námafjall sur la vallée de
        to the central volcano, Mt. Krafla.   Hlíðardalur et l'appareil volcanique de Krafla.

Blick vom Námafjall über das Tal Hlíðardalur
auf den Zentralvulkan Krafla.

Útsýni af Námafjalli yfir Hlíðardal til
megineldstöðvarinnar Kröflu.

4   Volcanic fissure at Leirhnjúkur in the central
    volcano, Mt. Krafla. It last erupted in 1984.

Fissure de Leirhnjúkur dans l'appareil volcanique de Krafla; le dernier épanchement de
lave date de 1984.

Vulkanspalte am Leirhnjúkur im Zentralvulkan
Krafla; letzter Ausbruch 1984.

Gossprunga við Leirhnjúk í Kröflu-megineld-
stöðinni; síðast virk 1984.

5   Hot springs in the high-temperature geother-mal area at Leirhnjúkur in the Mt. Krafla central volcano.

Sources chaudes dans la zone à haute température de Leirhnjúkur dans l'appareil volcanique de Krafla.

Heiße Quellen im Geothermalgebiet
Leirhnjúkur im Zentralvulkan Krafla.

Hverir á háhitasvæði við Leirhnjúk í Kröflu-
megineldstöðinni.

6   Goðafoss (15 m) in the Skjálfandi river.
     Folklore says that heathen idols were flung
     into the waterfall when the Icelanders adopt-
     ed the Christian religion in AD 1000.

La chute de Goðafoss (15 m) dans la rivière
Skjálfandi. L'histoire rapporte qu'on y jeta les
statues des dieux païens après l'adoption du
christianisme en AD 1000.

Der Goðafoss (15 m) im Fluß Skjálfandafljót.
Laut alter Sagen wurden dort nach der
Christianisierung Islands (AD 1000) heidnis-
che Götterbilder in den Wasserfall geworfen.

Goðafoss í Skjálfandafljóti (15 m). Segir
sagan að goðastyttum heiðins siðar hafi verið
kastað í fossinn eftir kristnitökuna árið 1000.

7   Dettifoss (44 m) in the Jökulsárgljúfur
National Park. The flow of water over the falls
is as much as 400-700 cubic metres per sec-
ond.

Dettifoss (44 m) dans le parc national de
Jökulsárgljúfur. En été le débit de la rivière
atteint souvent 400-700 m³ par seconde.

Der Dettifoss (44 m) im Nationalpark
Jökulsárgljúfur. Die Wassermenge im Sommer
kan bis 400-700 m³/Sek betragen.

Dettifoss (44 m) í þjóðgarðinum við
Jökulsárgljúfur. Á sumrin er rennsli árinnar
oft 400-700 rúmmetrar á sekúndu.

8 The stone pillars Karl (Old Man) and Kerling (Old Woman) are relics formed by erosion in the course of the river Jökulsá á Fjöllum in the Jökulsárgljúfur National Park.

Les rochers Karl et Kerling (le Vieux et la Vieille) ont résisté à l'érosion dans le lit de la rivière Jökulsá á Fjöllum, dans le parc national de Jökulsárgljúfur.

Die Felsen Karl og Kerling (Mann und Weib)
sind Reste eines alten Vulkanes im Bett der
Jökulsá á Fjöllum im Nationalpark
Jökulsárgljúfur.

Steindrangarnir Karl og Kerling eru rofleifar í
farvegi Jökulsár á Fjöllum í þjóðgarðinum við
Jökulsárgljúfur.

9 Columnar basalt in a thick layer of lava in the
   Jökulsárgljúfur canyon.

Colonnes de basalte dans l'épaisse couche de
lave dans le canyon de Jökulsárgljúfur.

Basaltsäulen in einer mächtigen Lavadecke in
der Schlucht Jökulsárgljúfur.

Stuðlaberg í þykku hraunlagi í
Jökulsárgljúfrum.

10   The Jökulsárgljúfur canyon is up to 150 m deep and 1-2 km across; it formed largely in a massive flood from the Vatnajökull glacier.

Le canyon de Jökulsárgljúfur atteint 150 m de profondeur sur 1 - 2 km de large; il s'est formé lors de crues cataclysmiques provenant du Vatnajökull.

Die Schlucht Jökulsárgljúfur ist bis zu 150 m
tief und 1-2 km breit. Sie entstand haupt-
sächlich während katastrophaler
Gletscherläufe aus dem Vatnajökull.

Jökulsárgljúfur eru allt að 150 m djúp og
1 - 2 km breið; aðallega mynduð í ham-
farahlaupum úr Vatnajökli.

11   Karlinn (the Old Man) at Langanes is a rock
      pillar that is home to cliff-nesting birds.
      Erosion by the sea has carved it from the
      bedrock.

Karlinn, le rocher aux oiseaux à la pointe de
Langanes, a resisté aux assauts du ressac
contre les falaises de la côte.

Der Vogelfelsen Karlinn an der Halbinsel
Langanes. Ein stummer Zeuge der gewaltigen
Kraft, mit der die Wellen des Nordatlantiks
gegen die Felsküste branden.

Fugladrangurinn Karlinn er við Langanes;
rofleif eftir átök brims við klettaströndina.

12   Hikers enjoy exploring the deserted regions of the East Fjords. Loðmundarfjörður in the mist.

Les zones inhabitées des fjords de l'est attirent les randonneurs. Vue sur Loðmundarfjörður qui se remplit de brume.

Die unbewohnten Fjorde an der Ostküste
Islands sind ein Wanderparadies. Blick über
den nebelverhangenen Loðmundarfjörður.

Óbyggðir við austfirsku firðina laða til sín
göngufólk. Séð yfir Loðmundarfjörð, hálf-
fullan af þoku.

13 Ice and fire. The Kverkfjöll volcano rises at the northern edge of the Vatnajökull glacier.

Feu et glace. Le massif volcanique de Kverkfjöll domine la lisière nord du Vatnajökull.

Feuer und Eis. Der Zentralvulkan Kverkfjöll ragt aus dem Nordrand des Gletschers Vatnajökull empor.

Ís og eldur. Megineldstöðin Kverkfjöll rís upp úr norðurjaðri Vatnajökuls.

14   The Markarfljótsgljúfur canyon is adjacent to one of Iceland's most-popular hiking routes, "Laugavegur" between Þórsmörk and Landmannalaugar.

Les gorges de Markarfljótsgljúfur sur l'un des grands sentiers de randonnées les plus fréquentés d'Islande entre Þórsmörk et Landmannalaugar, "Laugavegur".

Die Schlucht Markarfljótsgljúfur liegt am beliebtesten Weitwanderweg Islands, dem „Laugavegur" zwischen Þórsmörk und Landmannalaugar.

Markarfljótsgljúfur við vinsælustu, dagskiptu gönguleið á Íslandi; milli Þórsmerkur og Landmannalauga (Laugavegur).

15 The waterfall Dynkur in Þjórsá, Iceland's longest river (210 km).

La chute de Dynkur dans la Þjórsá, la plus longue rivière d'Islande (210 km).

Der Wasserfall Dynkur im längsten Fluß
Islands, der Þjórsá (210 km).

Fossinn Dynkur í Þjórsá, lengstu á Íslands
(210 km).

16 The Arctic riverbeauty (Chamaenerion lati-folium) at Krepputungur in the rain-shadow of the Vatnajökull glacier.

Épilobe arctique (Chamaenerion latifolium) dans les Krepputungur, à l'abri du Vatnajökull.

Arktische Weidenröschen (Chamaenerion lati-
folium) in den Krepputungur. Die Lavawüste
liegt im Regenschatten des Gletschers
Vatnajökull.

Eyrarrós (Chamaenerion latifolium) í
Krepputungum í úrkomuskugga Vatnajökuls.

17 Mt. Hekla (1,490 m) is Iceland's most famous, and most productive, volcano (eruptions in 1947, 1970, 1980, 1991).

L'Hekla (1490 m) est le volcan le plus connu et le plus productif d'Islande en même temps que son principal appareil volcanique (éruptions en 1947, 1970, 1980, 1991).

Die Hekla (1490 m) ist der bekannteste und produktivste Zentralvulkan Islands (Ausbrüche 1947, 1970, 1980, 1991).

Hekla (1490 m) er þekktasta og framleiðnasta eldfjall og megineldstöð Íslands (gos 1947, 1970, 1980, 1991).

18 Ljótipollur is a tephra crater formed in an explosive eruption, one of a series of eruptions in the Tungnaáröræfi region in 1480.

Ljótipollur (la vilaine mare) est un cratère d'explosion constitué de scories, qui date de la eruption explosive de Tungnaáröræfi en 1480.

Der Kratersee Ljótipollur befindet sich in einem Explosionskrater, der 1480 während einer Ausbruchsphase im Gebiet Tungnaáröræfi entstand.

Ljótipollur er gjóskugígur úr þeytigosi sem var hluti goshrinu á Tungnaáröræfum 1480.

19 Jökulgil near Landmannalaugar. Colourful gullies and gorges shaped by river erosion near the Torfajökull glacier.

Jökulgil près de Landmannalaugar. Les ravines et les gorges creusées par les cours d'eau du Torfajökull ont des coloris extraordinaires.

In der Schlucht Jökulgil bei Landmannalaugar. Die Schluchten und Klammen im
Torfajökulgebiet sind ungemein farben-
prächtig

Við Jökulgil hjá Landmannalaugum. Ársorfin
gil og gljúfur við Torfajökul eru afar litfögur.

20 High-temperature geothermal area at Zone géothermique à haute température de
    Mt. Brennisteinsalda, Landmannalaugar. Brennisteinsalda près de Landmannalaugar.

Ein Geothermalgebiet an der Brennisteinsalda
bei Landmannalaugar.

Háhitasvæði vð Brennisteinsöldu hjá
Landmannalaugum.

21 Hikers climbing Mt. Bláhnúkur in Land-mannalaugar, which commands panoramic views.

Randonneurs montant à Bláhnúkur, d'où l'on a le meilleur point de vue sur Landmannalaugar.

Wanderer beim Aufstieg zum Bláhnjúkur, dem
besten Aussichtsberg von Landmannalaugar.

Göngufólk á leið á Bláhnúk; helsta útssýnis-
stað við Landmannalaugar.

22 Mt. Eystrahorn (756 m) includes such rocks as gabbro. The mountain is a large magma intrusion, which has solidified in the earth's crust.

Sur Eystrahorn (756 m) on trouve des roches telles que du gabbro. La montagne est une infiltration de magma qui s'est solidifié dans l'écorce terrestre.

Im Eystrahorn (756 m) kann man Gesteinsarten wie Gabbro finden. Der Berg ist ein vulkanischer Intrusionskegel, der noch im Inneren der Erde erstarrte.

Í Eystrahorni (756 m) eru bergtegundir eins og gabbró. Fjallið er kvikuinnskot sem storknaði í jarðskorpunni.

23 Jökulsárlón is a glacial lagoon at the foot of the Breiðamerkurjökull glacier, which calves ice floes into the lagoon. The area of the lagoon is about 10 sq. km, and it is up to 170 metres in depth.

Le lagon de Jökulsárlón se trouve au pied de la langue glaciaire de Breiðamerkurjökull d'où se détachent des icebergs. Le lagon a plus de 10 km² et jusqu'à 170 m de profondeur.

Die Gletscherlagune Jökulsárlón befindet sich am Fuß der Gletscherzunge Breiðamerkur-jökull. Der Gletscher kalbt Eisberge in den 10 km² großen und bis zu 170 m tiefen See.

Jökulsárlón er undan Breiðamerkurjökli sem kelfir ísjökum í vatnið. Það er rúmir 10 km² og allt að 170 m djúpt.

24 Fjallsárlón lagoon and the icy face of the Fjallsjökull glacier. When the water freezes over, one can reach the snout of the glacier on foot.

Le lagon de Fjallsárlón et les falaises de glace du Fjallsjökull. Lorsque le lac est gelé, on peut aller à pied jusqu'au bord du glacier.

Der See Fjallsárlón und Eistürme am Gletscher
Fjallsjökull. Im Winter kann man manchmal
über den vereisten See bis ganz an die
Gletscherzunge herangehen.

Fjallsárlón og íshamrar Fjallsjökuls. Þegar
vatnið er ísilagt er unnt að ganga að jökul-
jaðrinum við lónið.

25   The church at Hof in the Öræfi district was
      built in 1883-1884 of timber, turf and rock.
      It is typical of the churches of old Iceland.

L'église de Hof dans l'Öræfasveit, bâtie en
bois, tourbe et pierres en 1883-84, est un
bon exemple de construction ancienne.

Die Kirche in Hof in Öræfi ist aus Holz, Torf und Steinen gebaut (1883-1884). Sie ist ein Beispiel für den Baustil isländischer Gottes-häuser aus den vergangenen Jahrhunderten.

Kirkjan að Hofi í Öræfasveit er byggð úr timbri, torfi og grjóti 1883-1884 og dæmi um guðshús fyrri tíma.

26   Mountain view in the Skaftafell National Park. The landscape is dominated by Iceland's largest volcano, Öræfajökull, and the country's highest peak (Hvannadalshnúkur, 2,119m, at the far right).

Vue sur les montagnes du parc national de Skaftafell, dominé par le plus grand volcan d'Islande, l'Öræfajökull, dont le pic Hvannadalshnúkur (2119 m) est le point culminant du pays (à l'extrême droite).

Panorama im Nationalpark Skaftafell. Der größte Vulkan Islands, Öræfajökull, mit dem höchsten Gipfel des Landes, Hvannadalshnjúkur (ganz rechts, 2119 m) dominiert den Blick.

Fjallasýn í þjóðgarðinum í Skaftafelli. Mest ber á stærsta eldfjalli Íslands, Öræfajökli, og hæsta tindi landsins (Hvannadalshnúk, 2119 m, lengst til hægri).

27 The Skaftafellsjökull outlet glacier flows from the Vatnajökull glacier. The stony ridge in the middle of the glacier consists of moraine eroded from the nunatak.

La langue glaciaire de Skaftafellsjökull descend du Vatnajökull. La moraine au milieu du glacier est formée de débris arrachés à la petite montagne.

Die Gletscherzunge Skaftafellsjökull fließt aus dem Vatnajökull herab. Die Moräne in der Mitte besteht aus Gesteinsschutt, den der Gletscher von den Felsen im Eis mitbringt.

Skaftafellsjökull fellur úr Vatnajökli. Urðarraninn í miðjum jökli er grjótmylsna sem jökullinn ber úr jökulskerinu.

28 Marshes and watermeadows below the Skaftafellsjökull glacier in the Skaftafell National Park.

Marécages et terres inondées devant le Skaftafellsjökull, dans le parc national de Skaftafell.

Moore und Sümpfe vor der Gletscherzunge
Skaftafellsjökull im Nationalpark Skaftafell.

Mýrlendi og flæður fyrir framan
Skaftafellsjökul í þjóðgarðinum í Skaftafelli.

29 The Svartifoss waterfall, in its setting of columnar basalt, is accessible by one of the park's many footpaths.

La cascade de Svartifoss dans son écrin de colonnes de basalte est accessible par un sentier du parc national de Skaftafell.

Der von Basaltsäulen umrahmte Wasserfall
Svartifoss liegt an einem Wanderweg im
Nationalpark Skaftafell.

Svartifoss í stuðlabergsumgjörð er við gönguleið í þjóðgarðinum í Skaftafelli.

30 Hvítárfoss waterfall, in the canyon at
Núpsstaðarskógar, not far from Skaftafell.

La chute de Hvítárfoss dans les gorges de
Núpsstaðarskógar, non loin de Skaftafell.

Der Wasserfall Hvítárfoss in den Schluchten
des Núpsstaðarskógar, nicht weit von
Skaftafell entfernt.

Hvítárfoss í gljúfrum við Núpsstaðarskóga,
skammt frá Skaftafelli.

31 Dyrhólaey. This headland was once an island, formed in a submarine volcanic eruption, and later joined to the mainland.

Dyrhólaey. Ce promontoire est en réalité les vestiges d'une ile née d'une éruption sous-marine et peu à peu reliée à la terre.

Dyrhólaey. Der Felsen ist der Rest einer Insel, die bei einem Vulkanausbruch im Meer entstand und später landfest wurde.

Dyrhólaey. Þessi höfði er í raun leif af eyju sem myndaðist í eldgosi í sjó en tengdist síðar landi.

32

Cloud formations over Mýrdalssandur. This 600 sq. km flood plain has been formed in the many eruptions of Mt. Katla. Capped by a glacier, Mt. Katla melts vast quantities of ice when it erupts, causing flash flooding.

Nuages au-dessus de Mýrdalssandur, vaste étendue de sables déposés sur 600 km² par les crues cataclysmiques dues aux maintes éruptions du volcan sous-glaciaire Katla.

Wolkenstimmung auf dem Mýrdalssandur. Der 600 km² große Sander wurde vom eisbedechten Vulkan Katla im Verlauf unzähliger Gletscherläufe geschaffen.

Skýjafar yfir Mýrdalssandi sem er 600 km² flóðslétta eftir fjölmörg Kötluhlaup.

33   Pétursey (284 m) is a volcano formed under
      the sea 120,00 to 300,000 years ago.

Pétursey (284 m) est un formation volcanique
qui s'est formé dans la mer il y a 120.000 à
300.000 ans.

Pétursey (284 m) entstand bei einem
Vulkanausbruch im Meer vor 120.000-300.000
Jahren.

Pétursey (284 m) er eldstöð sem varð til í sjó
fyrir 120.000-300.000 árum.

34 The Icelandic horse is at home in the chilly autumn breeze below the Eyjafjöll mountains.

Le cheval islandais est habitué aux frimas d'automne au pieds des montagnes d'Eyjafjöll.

Das Islandpferd fühlt sich im rauhen
Herbstwetter unter den Bergen Eyjafjöll zu
Hause.

Íslenski hesturinn er hagvanur í haust-
nepjunni undir Eyjafjöllum.

35 The farm of Hlíðarendi is well-known from the Saga of Njáll. Behind it lies the Eyjafjalla-jökull volcano (1,666 m) with its ice-cap.

La ferme de Hlíðarendi est connue depuis la saga de Njáll. Au fond se dresse le volcan d'Eyjafjallajökull coiffé d'un glacier (1666 m).

Der Bauernhof Hlíðarendi ist aus der Njáls-
saga bekannt. Im Hintergrund ragt der
vergletscherte Vulkan Eyjafjallajökull
(1666 m) auf.

Býlið Hlíðarendi er þekkt úr Njálu. Í baksýn
rís eldfjallið Eyjafjallajökull (1666 m) með
jökulhettu.

36 Geysisvæðið. Fremst er tvílitur hver sem heitir Blesi en í baksýn gýs Strokkur.

La zone de Geysir. Au premier plan, le bassin bicolore de Blesi et, au fond, une éruption du geyser Strokkur.

Das Gebiet des Großen Geysirs. Im Vordergrund eine zweifarbige heiße Quelle mit dem Namen Blesi, im Hintergrund ein Ausbruch des Geysirs Strokkur.

Geysissvæðið. Fremst er tvílitur hver sem heitir Blesi en í baksýn gýs Strokkur.

37   The Gullfoss waterfall (32 m) is one of the most popular tourist attractions in Iceland.

La chute de Gullfoss (32 m) est l'un des sites les plus visités des touristes en Islande.

Der Wasserfall Gullfoss (32 m) gehört zu den beliebtesten Attraktionen bei den Islandurlaubern.

Gullfoss (32 m) er einn vinsælasti áfangastaður ferðamanna á Íslandi.

38 All around Mt. Hekla are signs of volcanic activity. The red colour of the cinder is due to iron in the volcanic rock.

Les alentours d'Hekla portent la marque de l'activité volcanique. La couleur rouge des scories provient du fer des produits pyroclastiques.

Rund um die Hekla stößt man überall auf
Spuren des Vulkanismus. Die rote Farbe der
Schlacke kommt vom hohen Eisengehalt des
Vulkangesteins.

Umhverfi Heklu ber alls staðar merki eld-
virkni. Rauður litur á gjallinu stafar af járni
sem er í gosefnunum.

39   Iceland has a puffin (Fratercula arctica) population of 3-4 million. They are most common in the Westman Islands.

Il y a en Islande 3 à 4 millions de macareux (Fratercula arctica), dont la plupart nichent aux îles Vestmann.

Auf Island gibt es 3-4 Millionen Papageitaucher (Fratercula arctica). Am häufigsten sind sie auf den Westmännerinseln zu finden.

Á Íslandi eru 3-4 milljónir lunda (Fratercula arctica). Mest eru um þá í Vestmannaeyjum.

40

The Blue Lagoon is a popular bathing spa. The water, which has health-giving qualities, comes from far beneath the earth's surface at the Svartsengi geothermal power station.

Le Lagon Bleu est une baignade très appréciée. L'eau qui vient des entrailles de la terre près de la station géothermique de Svartsengi est bénéfique pour les maladies de la peau.

Die Blaue Lagune ist ein beliebter Badeort.
Das Wasser kommt aus dem Inneren der Erde
beim Geothermalkraftwerk Svartsengi und
besitzt Heilkräfte.

Bláa lónið er vinsæll baðstaður. Vatnið er
heilnæmt og komið úr iðrum jarðar við orku-
verið í Svartsengi.

Í iðnvæddum nútímasamfélögum man æ fleira fólk allt í einu eftir gömlum sannleika: Öll erum við hluti náttúrunnar; við verðum lifa af gæðum náttúrunnar í sátt við hana.

Eins og að líkum lætur sækja líka fleiri og fleiri kunnáttu og frið til náttúrunnar. Í mörgum iðnríkjanna þarf að leita vítt og breitt, og lengi, að nánum tengslum við náttúruna. Mannanna verk sjást víða á stórum svæðum. Má helst finna ósnortin víðerni langt í burtu; handan landamæra fjarlægra ríkja eða í afskekktum og strjálbýlum löndum.

Í Evrópu eykst mjög ásókn í fjölmörg náttúruverndarsvæði og sífellt færri, lítt snortin víðerni fara ekki varhluta af áhuga fólks á milliliðalausum samvistum við náttúruna. Í ljósi þessa er ekki að undra að jaðarlandið Ísland freisti fólks. Um helmingur þess eru öræfi með mörgum sjaldgæfum eða fögrum náttúruperlum. Stór, opin og lítt snortin svæði eru sem smyrsl á sál og líkama þess sem þeirra nýtur. Hinn hluti landsins, utan þéttbýliskjarna, er strjálbýl sveit með fjölbreyttri náttúru, bæði lifandi og lífvana.

Ísland er eitt yngsta landsvæði heims, séð með augum jarðfræðingsins. Landið er enn að myndast; eldgos verður fjórða hvert ár að jafnaði, og margs konar hverir bera frumkröftunum vitni í flestum landshlutum. Landið skelfur mörgum sinnum ár hvert og flekarekið skilur eftir sig ummerki; opnar sprungur og misgengi sjást víða í landslaginu. Um leið vinna útræn öfl á berggrunninum. Stórir jöklar vinna sitt verk ásamt ólmum straumvötnum, þungri úthafsöldu, gustmiklum vindum og tíðum skiptum milli frosts og þíðu. Allt þetta sjá menn greinilega á ferð um landið og eitt er víst: Náttúruváin gleymist vissulega ekki en Íslendingar hafa lært að lifa með henni og njóta landsins.

Land okkar er ekki aðeins óskaland þeirra sem gaman hafa af náttúrufegurð eða grjóti. Náttúran er lifandi og lífleg. Fagurgróin svæði með bjarkarskógum og litfögrum jurtum gleðja augað. Milljónir fugla sjást á flugi, einkanlega við strendurnar. Þar eru líka fjölmörg sjávarspendýr. Ár og vötn eru gjöfular veiði-slóðir en refir og hreindýr eigra um hálendið.

Það eru margar og góðar ástæður til þess að halda á vit náttúru og lands með öll skilningarvit opin og njóta þess sem við sækjumst æ meir eftir.